Shan

Biblical Reflections and
Pastoral Advice On Living with Shame

John Watson

Assistant Curate at Holy Trinity Richmond

GROVE BOOKS LIMITED
RIDLEY HALL RD CAMBRIDGE CB3 9HU

Contents

Acknowledgments

Thank you to all who have encouraged me in my thinking and writing and in 'trusting my own voice,' and with particular thanks to those who have shared with me their stories and experiences in their own journey towards acceptance and life.

First Impression March 2005
ISSN 0144-171X
ISBN 1 85174 588 2

Introduction—What is Shame? 1

'Shame is worse than death.' (Russian Proverb)

Dave[1] was sexually abused by his father at a young age. This event has deeply scarred his life, and though he is a Christian and has received counselling, prayer and various types of ministry, and would say very honestly that he has now forgiven his father, shame still raises its ugly, gnawing head and sometimes, at very unexpected moments. He says:

> Shame was and is the sense that I am in some way fundamentally bad or wrong and that everyone knows that or will find it out eventually.

It affects his relationship with close friends, questioning their friendship, and his relationship with his wife, questioning her love for him.

Susan is suffering from mental illness and is signed off from work. Each time she pays in her cheque at the bank, she feels the glower from the cashier and the silent condemnation 'there doesn't seem to be anything wrong with you—what are you receiving this for?' She cannot look the cashier in the face and wants to run away from this fortnightly horror.

Terry is young and unemployed. He is married and has a young family. They claim Housing Benefit to live in a small house in South London. He already lives with the private shame of not being able to find a good enough job to provide for his wife and small children. But he experienced public shame at the Housing Benefit office when his application was inspected—a group interview, all in suits, all mistrusting, all suspicious. 'I felt I needed to have a wash when I came out; I felt I was dirty, dishonest—all I wanted was someone to believe me.'

All of us have almost certainly experienced shame at one time or another, whether it was being 'found out' or because of other people's actions upon us. The phrase 'shame on you!' produces a number of emotions and responses. Shame is an intensely private, yet at the same time an extremely public emotion. It is private because it is usually concerned with things that we want to hide from others (and at a deeper level ourselves as well) and public because when we are found out it is in the excruciatingly painful view of others, seeing us for who we *really* are. Shame is played out in the public playground and it begins at an early age from the taunts of children as they see their classmate

3

with wet shorts and a small puddle around their feet to the bruised face of a woman suffering from domestic violence, desperately trying to hide what has happened. It is a primitive, undeniable and strong presence in the human psyche.

Yet it is also a very 'unfashionable virtue'[2] in modern Western society for it suggests that 'we are no good' and so we try to banish it. We know it exists but we often want to deny it. In fact in some cases, and unfortunately the church often colludes with this, we are actually discouraged from acknowledging it, not because of any malicious attempts at covering it up but because shame has not been articulated enough in the public realm to allow such acknowledgment. As a result it festers because we are not in a position to deal with it. It lies dormant but niggling away every so often and occasionally raises its head like a hidden terrorist to wreck the peace and relative order of our lives.

The aim of this book is to explore the effects of shame and what pastoral responses there may be to 'set people free' from the harmful effects of shame and lead us to a place where shame can play its part in our journey of faith.

Good? Bad? Or Just Plain Uncomfortable?

Many contemporary writers and therapists regard shame as always being negative. It 'devalues the soul' and prevents the true potential of someone being realized. Yet some people may be surprised to hear that not all shame is bad.

Positive or 'healthy' shame can prevent immoral or harmful behaviour. If someone is at a point in their life when they feel they could commit an act of adultery, feelings of shame may emerge before an affair has begun, as the person is thinking about the effects it may have on those closest to him or her and the effects it will have on him- or herself as an individual. In this case shame acts as a way of preventing a certain type of action. It protects the boundaries between us and other people, reminding us that we are relational beings, because shame is a relationally based feeling.

Shame also protects our spiritual relationship with God, reminding us that we are spiritual beings. The Talmud reads 'A sense of shame is a lovely sign in a man. [sic] Whoever has a sense of shame will not sin so quickly.'[3]

Yet many also experience the intensely negative or 'unhealthy' aspects of shame, where the self is assessed, often negatively, where the spiral of negative assessment becomes 'the disintegration of the self.'[4] For most people its effects can be disabling, preventing them from 'living life to the full' (John 10.10). It is to these effects which we now turn.

The Effects of Shame

2

Physical Effects

Shame can be an intensely painful feeling that can shudder throughout the body. The English word for *shame* has its roots in an Indo-European word *kam/ kem*, which means to cover, to hide. Many images of shame usually present the figure, hiding, crouching, cowering, trying to cover itself, seeking to become smaller or invisible. This is not just out of embarrassment but out of a desire to be distant and in reaction to inner feelings of self-disgust, whether this is the anorexic reviling at her image in the mirror or the adult recovering from child abuse. If the person is not actually physically presenting these effects, he or she is probably experiencing them inwardly. Our bodies communicate publicly what we long to hide. Signs of shame may include:

- involuntary blushing
- hunched shoulders
- head bent towards the ground
- no eye contact

My feeling of shame is a cloak that lives under the skin — very visible and thin'

As someone once told me 'my feeling of shame is a cloak that lives under the skin — very visible and thin.'

When I worked as a student pastor in South London, I once encountered a woman at church who had been suffering ongoing verbal and physical abuse from her ex-husband. As I offered some support for her and her children, she started sharing feelings of self-disgust and unworthiness — the raw and heavy cloud of long-term depression was very present. She often could not look me in the face when explaining things to me and her body language all spoke of utter rejection and the fear of being rejected again. Whilst one has to be careful about jumping to conclusions, the visible and outward indicators were pointing very clearly to that which was being experienced inwardly. In the case of this suffering woman, shame was dwelling just beneath the skin and was affecting and infecting how she was seeing herself.

Psychological Effects

Jean-Paul Sartre sees shame as how somebody feels when they suddenly see themselves in the eyes of another.[5] Shame is a feeling that involves an 'other,' whether that is in the public realm or the internalized sense of self that is held up in the mind of the individual. We know the 'shoulds' and the 'oughts' of behaving, being, believing, acting and saying and we are faced with our failures before others or ourselves. This could be the vicar of a church who has not seen the numbers of people he or she had hoped come flooding into the building. Great expectations may have been communicated to the congregation or to the bishop and to colleagues with amazing amounts of enthusiasm and confidence. These expectations were at first 'inside,' driving this person towards what was felt should be done, so not seeing the great numbers come in is a real disappointment in this person's own eyes but it becomes catastrophic when, in the eyes of others, the 'failure' has been noted. This aspect of shame as being seen, whether by real or imaginary eyes, turns our *self* into an object. We are the ones being scrutinized by the hard eyes of others. We are the ones under the microscope of inspection, not just what we are doing. Michael Lewis writes 'In shame we become the object as well as the subject of shame.'[6] The focus is not on specific actions, but on the self as 'who I am.'

The focus is not on specific actions, but on the self as 'who I am'

When we experience unhealthy shame, we encounter a crisis of identity. Shamed people feel worthless, empty, or hollow. Masks may be adopted to protect their vulnerability, trying to be someone or something they are not, putting more pressure on the sense of identity. In a simple but highly poignant example, the American reality TV show *Extreme Makeover* offers the participants to change who they are by cosmetic surgery, because they feel ugly. Their sense of who they are, when compared to the 'oughts' and 'shoulds' of society, is not good. 'You ought to be like this, you should be like that' are pressures we all face. These pressures can shape a person unhealthily, directing them into a way of seeing themselves in an ever descending spiral of shame with the thoughts 'I am no good' being drilled deep into their being.

Spiritual Effects

So where is the image of God in all this complexity and fragility? Often the person living with unhealthy shame sees God as the accuser, not the healer. God is not the one who can restore but is the silent judge in the background, glaring with a disapproving shake of the head. God is not the one who listens; he is removed and uninterested in the plight of people. The eyes of God are either burning into the vulnerable soul or turned away in disgust. We

6

cannot approach God if we are such people. The wrath of God or the fear of God—what will he say, what will he do—is so uppermost in the minds of the person coping with shame and the bad self-image that this generates, that any thought of God as accepting and loving is lost. Worm theology is very prevalent in the minds of shamed people. They hardly need reminding of the depravity of humanity and the wretchedness of themselves.

This person does not need to hear that she is not worthy— she needs to hear that she is accepted and welcomed, trusted and loved

I once took home communion with a woman who suffers from depression and a very low sense of identity. I used the prayer of humble access 'We do not presume…' and suddenly realized as we said the words 'we are not worthy…' that this person does not need to hear that she is not worthy—she needs to hear that she is accepted and welcomed, trusted and loved, that there is someone who believes in her and is with her, not far removed from her and approachable only if we say the right words.

So how do we help the person who may have these feelings of shame? How do we help the person who is so shaped by shame that they see God as one who wants to punish all the time? I will look at more spiritual implications and offer suggestions in dealing with shame later in this book, but first we need to look at how shame differs from guilt—two closely connected emotions.

3

Shame and Guilt

'I feel guilty' one may say, 'but I am my shame.' [7]

In our own experiences the two feelings of shame and guilt happen together and often in our own mind we cannot separate them. Some people think that shame is the same as guilt. Maybe this is the fault of our own church traditions. Someone once said that we learn our theology by the songs we sing; if this is the case, there is not too much around to teach us about these feelings. When we do sing songs about guilt and forgiveness it is usually just that—there is no mention of shame. The language tends only to focus on the image of guilt being washed clean away like specks or lumps of dirt on a clean white garment (forgiveness) so that that it can become bright shiny and white again—only to be soiled in a few days' time. This repeated cycle of washing—which would normally make the toughest pair of jeans a bit threadbare—does not seem to be able to get at the root of the staining, only the stain itself. It does not address the feeling that a shamed person may be experiencing. Of course there are beautiful images of this cleansing and refreshing in the Bible and we all need to own them and experience the cleansing power of God's grace. But there are other aspects of God's deep work in our lives that we need to hear and re-tell, to fashion us and address what is actually going on. A focus simply on guilt will not do that. But first we need to understand what guilt and shame are.

> *This repeated cycle of washing does not address the feeling that a shamed person may be experiencing*

Guilt

Is there such a thing as 'good' guilt? How can guilt—one of those words which contains all sorts of images like a wolf tearing into the flesh—ever be good? I mean, Jesus came to free us from guilt did he not? Well yes—of course, but without guilt we could be doing all sorts of things. Like a healthy aspect of shame, mentioned earlier, at its basic level guilt has its place in helping to prevent wrong behaviour but also signalling to us that there is something wrong. The problems come when this feeling is tied up with numerous other aspects of who we are or what has happened without this feeling being explored further. In our society, we tend to make judgments about guilty/not guilty as an instant reaction to an event, or 'feel guilty' when we feel bad or *s when our instinctive action is to feel 'guilty' that we need to unpack what that really is*

wrong. It is when our instinctive reaction is to feel guilty that we need to unpack what that really is. Many times we feel guilty when it is not our fault—this is false guilt.

Whether it is 'true' guilt where we have committed a sin or 'false' guilt, where we assume guilt which is not ours to own (for example, in the case of being abused where we may say 'But I must have done something that made him or her abuse me') the *feeling* of guilt is apparent. I *feel* guilty about actions that I have *done* or actions that others have *done to* me. When it comes to sorting out what is 'true' and what is 'false' guilt the counsellor may want to identify who committed the deed or action that led to the feelings of guilt. If there is something to be confessed, then the true guilt can be dealt with by some form of liturgical confession. This type of guilt is easier to name, own and remedy. In an action based society, such confession and absolution can be helpful.

Our penal system is based on focussing on the crime or wrong deed and punishing it. Through this punishment the offender is hopefully going to say sorry at the end. Sometimes of course, for certain crimes, we just want to see the offender punished, and have little interest in whether they say sorry at all. Here guilt is not just a feeling but a state. You are guilty of the action. You need to suffer the consequences, as the law determines.

This is taken into our theology and ideas about God and who we are. We *are* guilty, not just *feeling* guilty, and hence open to the judgment of God. But the death of Christ has now enabled God to pronounce 'not guilty' on those who confess their sins.

The person may then experience cleansing from God and feel white as snow. But if there is actually nothing to be confessed, because 'I did nothing wrong,' that is, the guilt is 'false,' then confession will not work. If 'true' guilt was present and has been confessed but the feeling of badness remains, then we need to move towards something else. If actually what is at the heart of our actions and behaviour, our sense of who we are, is not our human state of guilt but something else, then we

We need a biblically based metaphor to help articulate what is going on

need another language to help express that something else. We need a biblically based metaphor to help articulate what is going on. In a church tradition that has exaggerated the penal theory of atonement, such a metaphor is needed to balance the images and ideas that convey the work of Christ as simply taking our punishment. A focus on shame can help to address that.

Shame

Most observers on the subject see the division in a simple but helpful way:

◆ *guilt* derives its feelings from wrongdoing, what one *does* or *says*;

◆ *shame* is about whom one *is*. This diagram may help in showing the differences:[8]

SHAME (Focus on the self)	GUILT (Focus on the act)

What is wrong?	
Failure to meet expectations	Offence against legal expectations

Personal Reaction	
Embarrassment / Disgrace Self-deprecation Fear of abandonment Resentment Self-isolation Alienation	Condemnation / Remorse Self-accusation Fear of punishment Anger Self-justification Hostility

Reaction of others	
Exclude and ridicule Disgrace and hold in contempt Disapprove and reproach	Blame and hold responsible Accuse and condemn Punish and retaliate

How to remedy the state / feeling	
Learn to see 'who I am' in relation to others	Pay the price, then you will be restored
Love banishes shame	Justification banishes guilt

Shame focuses on seeing the person as bad. Guilt sees the bad action, sometimes by a bad person.

Whilst on placement in a prison during my training for ordained Anglican ministry, I encountered the case of a female prisoner who sexually assaulted and murdered her own children. The case shocked me immensely and I was surprised, yet full of admiration, at the way the Catholic chaplain was able to meet with her, to counsel her and prepare her for a time of Confession, which incidentally was at the inmate's request. The appalling act, which she recognized for herself, led to terrific amounts of guilt (hating what she had done) and shame (hating her very self). The Confession helped towards dealing with the guilt yet the shame needed to be dealt with in order for her to be healed completely. If she was ever to arrive at a place in her life where she could raise her head again, the chronic element of shame needed to be addressed. It later transpired that she too had been abused and as a result of being unable to deal with the feelings that had been generated, the shame she had experienced became rage towards others. I imagine that there will always be an element of shame within her, but the aim of the Chaplain was to see that this was manageable, that she could reach a place where she could come to terms with herself instead of living with self-hate and self-harm.

This example helps show the differences between guilt and shame. The very fact that she was in prison is a response to her being guilty. Clearly she did wrong. She was being punished out of a belief that as long as she 'does the time' or 'pays the price' she could be restored. But if she is ever to come to a place where she can forgive herself, to be fully restored, and live with the knowledge that she is loved by God despite what she did, she needs to deal with the shame of what happened, and ultimately with the shame that is deep within her, caused by what happened to her. Often where the guilt can be dealt with, feelings of unworthiness and badness remain—here the issue is shame.

Shame does not respond to punishment. We only have to look at the results of the prison population to see that punishment does not work—with over 71% of young offenders being re-convicted. Where does punishment lead? It leads to more sin and shame, not to healing and restoration.

When There is No Guilt

Though the above case is an extreme one, the feelings of shame can be just as intense as those experienced by people who feel shame for what has happened *to them*—where people have been abused or do not fit in to a group or society, or who have been shaped by shame over a long period of time. Here there is no 'true' guilt; they do not need to hear words of forgiveness but words of healing. Absolution is not required but acceptance is.

Shame has its place in social conditioning and our sense of belonging. It is to this which we now turn.

Absolution is not required but acceptance is

4   Shame, Identity and Society

Shame is implicitly linked to identity.

We have already seen that it is 'me' who is under the microscope of inspection—not just what I do. So the issue of shame is always about how I see myself and how I want others to see me. This is often linked to actions and behaviour, but also to values and ethics, and often to what we are expected to be.

Home is Where the Heart is

David Ford in *The Shape of Living* uses the phrase 'community of the heart'[9] to help us see how we come to understand the key question 'Who am I?' This is where we think of the people that have been involved in our lives. He writes:

> Our most powerful feelings relate to them, feelings such as love, anger, jealousy, hatred, rivalry, gratitude, hero worship, status seeking, and urge to dominate. A big part of our inner life is taken up with people, and they loom large in our memories, fantasies, and hopes…The heart is like a home for all the concerns of our lives, where our identity is sorted out year after year.[10]

Our heart, the place for a myriad of meetings, with people past and present, is where we remember events, conversations, words all attached to people—our own 'community' or 'home.' In fact, the very language we use about ourselves, which describes who we are, is learned from others.

Sometimes though, 'home life' is not as safe and secure as we always want it. There can be moments of fun and peace, where love helps to raise self-esteem and belief. But others are places where divorce has harmed, or domestic violence and abuse has bruised and injured.

As in the real tragedies of home life, the home of our hearts can also continue to carry those memories and events, rusting away any sense of self-belief and hope. Our heart becomes wounded. Where those relationships have threatened us— either by rejection of a close friend or a group within society—'we feel the weave of our self with others is unravelling or being torn.'[11] Our sense of who we are is shaped by the various encounters of the past and present that reside in the home of our heart.

Some studies by Erik Erikson on the human lifecycle confirm what Ford is saying, linking shame to childhood development and the sense of personal identity. This is important as Erikson also sees identity as being 'psychosocial'[12] where our sense of 'who we are' and place in the world is linked to what is going on around us. In a changing world and in a society in a state of flux, people are searching for something. People are searching for security and a sense of belonging. Let us look at it this way:

- Life in a council estate is very different from life in a leafy suburb — the messages you receive from the neighbours can affect how you behave and see yourself.

- You move jobs and suddenly expectations are greater — these will affect what you do and how you want others to see you.

- You go to church and hear how you should live your life — these voices will affect how you see yourself and your place in that group of people. Your actions will be judged, too, in the light of what is accepted behaviour.

We interact with these expectations, our social environment, our 'community of the heart' and in reaction we may feel shame at times for not living up to those expectations — like the person with a mental illness who does not fit into what are 'accepted' ways of living.

Shame has a way of polluting the heart. Our whole 'community' is affected — it changes how we are seen in our own eyes and in the eyes of others. When this pollution enters the 'home' we:

- seek to *escape* from the environment, to an inward and lonely world;

- *lose touch with others*, because the other has been harmful, so we lose social bonds because they have been wounding;

- then lose a real sense of self, because we *do not trust* ourselves anymore.

Ministering to someone whose heart is so wounded involves helping them to see the main characters in the community of the heart, those healthy ones and those who have committed harm — our significant characters. The heart needs to be transformed by those wounds and where before there may have been defensive walls erected to protect, these can be dismantled as we offer hospitality once more.

I Shop Therefore I Am

But there is a larger, more pervasive and downright crippling expression of shame in the 21st century British society that helps shape who we are. We live in a consumer society. We are all consumers—we cannot avoid that. We are all asked to partake in the great choice-fest of daily visits to the supermarkets or shopping malls. We are daily persuaded that this or that shirt, mobile, food, house or car will make us a better person, will help us be part of a group. We shop in order to be. A recent advert used the language of shame explicitly: 'Ashamed of your mobile?' The subtext reads: then you need to be like the rest of us and walk around with the latest model. The pressure to have the 'good life' is extreme. The pressure to have the best trainers, to wear the latest jacket,

A recent advert used the language of shame explicitly: 'Ashamed of your mobile?'

to drive the 'best' car, to own the latest gadget, to go on the flashiest holiday, to live in the best parts of the town or city, is all very evident and all a statement of how we want others to see who we are. If you have the cash to do it, you are fine, but what if not? British consumer debt is now over £1 trillion. The weight and burden of debt on already poor people is massive. Why? Because if they do not partake in this they will feel excluded and shamed.

The Government phrase 'social exclusion' embodies all that is experienced by people who 'fail' to be consumers, or as one sociologist puts it, the 'new poor.'[13] They cannot be part of the system because they do not have the money to allow them to be part of it. They cannot be true consumers—they are excluded. Contemporary advertizing utilizes the feelings of shame in an attempt to manipulate the actions and choices of the consumer, who is in the context of seeking an identity and sense of belonging, within this consumer society. You either belong or you do not.

There are social ills to be avoided too—unemployment, debt (though interestingly 'credit' is a good thing), poverty, mental illness, being a refugee or asylum seeker, homelessness. If you happen to be affected by one of these groups then you will know what it feels like. Shunned, disregarded, shamed. Imagine what this does to a person's own sense of worth and feelings?

Those who are excluded need to feel empowered and accepted if this type of shame is to be overcor

Shame is far more to do with feelings of powerlessness—feeling shy, inhibited, weak, helpless and often on the other end of a power relationship. Ridicule and humiliation add to the already present disempowering feelings. Those who are excluded need to feel empowered and accepted if this type of shame is to be overcome.

Each Sunday we come to church, a community of faith, with all these pressures and expectations ringing more loudly in our ears than the toll of the bell or the strumming of the guitar calling us to worship. It is in the context of the church that the struggle between the very many expectations of 'who I am to be' and 'what I am to do' is played out, because often we have a whole number of voices and influences all calling us to be this or that. And if we do not or cannot meet those expectations we may feel shame at who we are. So it is therefore the context of the church which must offer help and direction to those of us who struggle with what it means to 'be' in a very fragmented and sometimes disordered society.

The need to address feelings of shame, particularly where it is unhealthy and misplaced, is also the calling of the church and the ministry of the gospel. What does the Bible say about shame and about how God addresses the issues that shame has? What other language and metaphors are there to help express God's love and acceptance of the shamed person rather than imposing a sense of wrath and rejection that they are already experiencing? We will go on to consider these questions in the next chapter.

5

Shame and the Bible

As we look into the biblical examples of shame, it is worth remembering that the Bible was written in and for a communal culture, rather than the far more individualized Western one we find ourselves in today.

Any references to shame cannot simply be read on an individual basis only. This becomes even more important in the light of the social aspects of shame in today's society.

It is also important to be aware of the images of God we present in interpreting biblical passages. Our images of God often tell us more about ourselves than about God, revealing how we see ourselves and how we see others. It is vital when trying to understand the biblical evidence for shame that we try to be honest about how we have come to understand God—about the influences, both social and psychological, that have shaped how we see God to be. In part, an investigation into God and shame in the Bible is also an investigation into who we are and how we react. A pastor and theologian must never forget that.

Adam and Eve

This is the classic story of how sin estranged humanity and God. Traditionally it is often interpreted in the light of the sinful and therefore guilty state that human beings now find themselves in because of their own sin. Yet the story also shows the shame experienced as a result of sin. The responses of Adam and Eve show that shame is a very present reality as well as guilt. The responses of God reveal how he deals with both.

The following is a short reflection on the passage and events surrounding the Fall, with a particular emphasis on the presence of shame.

Walking Tall

The first mention of the word 'shame' in the Bible occurs in Genesis 2.25, referring to Adam and Eve when they do not feel any shame in their naked state. This is not simply referring to a lack of embarrassment at having no clothes on, but as a sign that they were completely accepting of each other and themselves, with an open and free relationship between themselves and God. They could 'walk tall,' confident in who they were. We have all seen people that ooze this type of confidence—able to try anything, be themselves with anyone, no pretences. More often than not, these people know deep down that they are loved—by their parents, partner or God. Adam and Eve can look at one another and at God, exposed and vulnerable, yet accepting and non-threatening. As in the early years of a child, who will happily dance in front of you in merry abandonment, unaware they may not have a stitch on, Adam and Eve walk, talk, play and be all that they are—in the knowledge that they are accepted.

Later childhood years reveal a sense of modesty, which moves on to teen-age years when we become aware of inspecting eyes which judge and make statements that we hear or perceive. These judgments threaten our sense of who we are, our sense of being *happy* with who we are. If the foundations of love have been rocked, this period of life where judgments and perceptions of what 'others' are saying may result in a lack of self-esteem and worth. It may till the ground where the seeds of shame grow into unhealthy weeds which seek to wrap around our legs and smother us. Adam and Eve walk in the confidence that they are loved.

Acting Small
Yet as life moves on challenges come our way. Things happen to us or we make the wrong choices. In all the freedom that God has given us in life we have the freedom to do wrong too. The freedom he has placed with us is a sign of trust and belief in us. It is when we break that trust, when we choose to sin, the results of that sin occur. It is when Adam and Eve disobey God, and fear the gaze of God after they disobey, that they hide and cover themselves up (3.6–13). This inner confidence disappears; they crouch and hide, they do not want to see God, they do not want to look him in the eyes—all classic expressions of coping with shame, fear and guilt. They have not just betrayed God—they have betrayed themselves too. They are aware now of what *he* might say or *do* because of what *they* have *done*, but more than this they are aware now how bad they must *be*. They are too afraid to encounter him—and rightly so, for he had said that they would die if they ate of that tree. When we sin there are feelings of guilt and shame and sometimes fear. What do we say when we minister to people who have sinned? Do they fear the reaction of God like Adam and Eve? Do they still live in the grip of that fear—of what he will do to them? And how do they feel about themselves? Do we leave them squirming and hiding? I think sometimes there is a reaction in us that wants to see them squirm and wriggle and feel bad. They deserve it—it is a sort of punishment. If this is so, then where does the healing and forgiveness come from? By whom is the call to accept yourself given?

God's Call

God responds to their disobedience but not in the way they expected. The miracle is that Adam and Eve do not die; they still live. Guilt is present and God deals with it. But what we also see is a relationship broken down. Mistrust enters, breaking apart that which was once close and intimate. In any relationship when things go wrong, there is a period of grief and mistrust, doubt and fear, insecurities and feelings of abandonment. God's relationship with his children is in danger of breaking apart. Amazingly we see God searching for those he loves—seeking for those who are hiding. Calling for them, waiting for them to respond. Is God the harsh Victorian father figure who will beat his children with a belt? The judge who will condemn the guilty? As Adam and Eve respond we almost picture small children, with their fingernails poised at their teeth, feeling small and unsure, unaware of the seamstress God who is busy helping to clothe them. Words are spoken and the results of mistrust and sin are felt and spelled out (vv 15–17) but the actions of a loving God seek to restore the relationship, helping to rebuild the love that was between them. As in a marriage that is breaking apart, the first steps of love are essential to build trust and confidence again.

In the act of clothing the nakedness (v 21) God initiates healing and restoration, helping them to be who they are despite what they have done. In their experience of shame, which has come out of an act of disobedience, God moves to help them feel less ashamed. He shows that he *still accepts* them and *loves* them, that they are of value and worth caring for, despite their disobedience. God does not reject them or disown them or say 'get out of my sight.'

Though the story is often remembered for this one case of disobedience, the call of God to live in all that he has given and celebrate the goodness and freedom of creation is also of equal importance. For the God who prohibits is also the God who invites and permits life in his creation. That life must have boundaries, however.[14] God moves the couple on and deals with their shame—he clothes them, for they cannot clothe themselves or each other, and in that clothing they are given life. In that act of clothing he still offers protection and nurture. Through our own life when things happen to us, when things seem to be collapsing around us, our God, who still loves and accepts us, is still 'clothing' us. We cannot meet the needs of our own shame; shame needs to be healed by others demonstrating their love for us. This has practical implications which we will look at in the last chapter.

Adam and Eve are given an opportunity to continue living in that call and freedom of God. But now they are touched by life a little bit more, aware of what the call to freedom implies—living with the results of choosing the wrong thing. They are not forgotten, but are loved and still protected.

How much more so is this message of love and acceptance needed for those who had things done to them, for those who were sexually or physically abused, or for the person who suffers as a result of simply being somebody who has disabilities or is not accepted for who they are? God's call is still being offered—God's nurturing and protection is still available.

Other Old Testament References

Shame was used as a way to help bring a unity to a nation and to ensure people did the right thing. It focussed on the person rather than just the act. A certain type of activity or event would bring shame on a community—therefore there were strict ways of behaving. Often public punishment was meant to help restore the shamed person into relationships again, but there were categories of behaviour that would mean permanent exclusion. This is not unlike the 'honour' crimes that have hit headlines in the UK recently, doubling in the last four years. Most honour crimes involve women deemed to have dishonoured their family or community. In Old Testament times strict codes of conduct are observed that keep relationships at the forefront of social cohesion.

References to the word 'shame' in the Old Testament tend to focus on:

- Ritual purity and ideas of cleanness—a wide tapestry of taboos and wrong acts. Shame is experienced as a feeling and a state of being when you or your family are excluded from the community (issue of blood—Lev 12; no children—Deut 25). Being shamed or disgraced had dire consequences for the person, family or tribe concerned, and these consequences had religious overtones.
- Shame acts as a preventative—it acts to stop immoral behaviour, because the consequences are huge. Those who act without any shame are the ones who are most condemned. 'You refuse to be ashamed' (Jer 3.3).
- There is a fear of being alienated from God as a result of sin. 'Do not cast me away from your presence' (Psalm 51.11).
- Shame is a reaction for failing to keep the covenant with God (Jer 3.24–25).

The Pros...

In many ways our society is very different from that of the Old Testament. The great strength of the Old Testament community and vision of social care was to see people as part of the whole, not isolated individuals fighting for their own rights and positions. The positive side was to help keep some boundaries around life—not everything was good and beneficial. Shame helped people see they were connected to others, that the community life was the way to help others and not just themselves.

...and the Cons

The weakness was that there was a pressure to conform—and usually conform to the wishes of those in power. Shame was therefore used to ensure people did what the powerful wanted, and not just what was right. The negative side of shame was open to be used as an oppressive force. The threat of exclusion hung heavy over people and the realities of exclusion are seen in the people Jesus encountered and ministered amongst.

Yet though we claim we are an individualist society, we still use shame in a number of situations to ensure people act properly; individuals are 'named and shamed' to make sure they suffer as a result of doing something wrong. If people do not fit our way of thinking in our own groups we tend to exclude them.

We also feel shame in our relationship with God—if we sin, we feel we cannot be loved or even accepted. This idea that only if we say certain words will we be accepted again is emphasized in prayers and sometimes sermons. This 'natural' way of seeing the results of sin bypasses what has been seen in Adam and Eve, and also what we see in the life of Jesus.

Shame in the New Testament

The gospels bring a wider understanding of the issue of shame. Jesus meets and ministers to people who have been rejected as a result of a culture that has strict rules on how to *do* things right. If you happened to *be* someone who was regarded as poor, a sinner or diseased, you were outside; not just your actions—but you.

'It's not your fault'

The encounter of Jesus with the women who has been bleeding for many years (Luke 8.43–48) is one of many beautiful and powerful examples of Jesus over-riding the social norms of the day.[15] This woman, according to Levitical law, was a social outcast, cut off from any religious life due to her uncleanness. She would feel shamed by her own condition which would be exacerbated by the public shunning and shaming of her. The power of the majority here is to set the norms and thereby state who is included. The power of the story is that Jesus overrides these norms.

The account reminds us that Jesus' interaction with the woman breaks the rules and expectations of the day. People would have been shocked to hear this—for Jesus is not simply addressing the issue of healing, but of social acceptance, offering new possibilities of human life and community. Jesus' public acceptance of her is a ministry to her sense of self as well as a healing of her body. Mark stresses the word 'touch' four times (5.27–31) so the woman is restored socially as well as physically. St Francis saw the touching of the leprous as one of the deepest acts of love and acceptance that could be shown to another ostracized and shamed group. When Princess Diana touched AIDS patients she crossed a taboo and helped overcome misconceptions, helping them find dignity and feel included again. Jesus is actually subverting the cleansing system and declaring himself to be the one that cleanses. Jesus is quite clearly saying, 'It's not your fault. I accept you as you are.'

There are a number of 'reversals' occurring within the context of this encounter and Jesus going to minister to the synagogue leader's daughter (Mark 5.21–43).

- Jairus—a man who has a name.
- The Woman—has no name.

- Jairus—one of the leaders of the synagogue who has status, position, power and perhaps money.
- The Woman—has nothing, no status, no power, no money.

- Jairus—the head of his family, stands up for his daughter.
- The Woman—no family, no-one to stand up for her.

- Jairus—approaches in full public view with confidence, falling at Jesus' feet.
- The Woman—sneaks up trying to hide.

- Jairus—asks Jesus to lay hands on his daughter.
- The Woman—secretly touches.

Someone from the bottom of the social heap intrudes on a mission to someone who is at the top.[16] There is also a reversal in the Beatitudes (Matt 5.1–11) where the traditional groups who would feel shame, like the poor, the meek and the hungry are given the highest status and acceptance.

Jesus not only heals the condition of the woman, but challenges the system that caused her the shame and rejection. He publicly accepts her and ministers to her shame but also, in doing that, attacks the structures that were in existence. This 'parabolic healing'[17] and others like it function to unmask the powerful structures of the day. Jesus did this in many encounters with the poor, the diseased and the 'sinners.' He belonged to those who had been pronounced 'accursed' (John 7.49). He shared the stigma of their inferiority and was equally excluded.

Shame as a Way of Life?
Mary actually faced public shame and humiliation by accepting God's call upon her life. She knew what was happening, but others did not. You can imagine the whispers: 'How can he marry her now? It cannot be his surely!' In a culture highly dependent on moral honour, it seems a strange way for God

the Father to introduce the world to his Son! Conceived out of wedlock, in a lowly town on the outskirts, Jesus' own sense of worth was not in what others said of him but in what God his Father said of him (Matt 3.17). Through that sense of identity, he was able to change others' perceptions of who they were. He calls us to be born again, to change our self-image based on him, who is the image of the invisible God, so that this image may be re-born within us.

The gospels show Jesus accepting the shame of crucifixion—a death for the underclass, slaves and foreigners. Jesus was taken out of the city, excluded from the community, publicly exposed, shamed and disgraced. Perhaps in fact there is no wrath of God being poured out at the cross, but identification with our sin and shame and an overcoming of our sin and shamefulness. The anguished love, which is expressed though his solidarity with us, banishes our shame.

Christ's life is our life. His call is our call. Our ministry is to embrace those who are called shameful, to express love and acceptance, not condemnation and punishment of the person.

- We are called to overcome taboos with our own lives, to reveal the love and image of God within each person we encounter.
- We are called to preach a message which emphasizes love and healing, not punishment and death.
- We are called to be a model for others of the love and life of God and all that he offers. Life to the full can be found, but only if it is expressed and felt.

This means we need to be very careful in how we preach and pray. We need to look at the language and theology in our songs and prayers, sermons and services, that we do not inadvertently blow out that smouldering wick or break that bruised reed. The person coping with unhealthy shame is a very vulnerable person.

It also means that we need to look seriously at our own lives and that of those around us.

For Further Reflection

- What influences are there which speak to us about who we are?
- What forces and structures in society seek to shape us and mould us, as they sought to shape and mould the woman suffering from uncontrolled bleeding?
- Society is the environment in which we live our faith. What things do we need to be aware of, in order to open our eyes and see what is happening?

A Way Forward 6

I have already hinted at some things which need to change if shame is to be addressed within the church at an appropriate level.
This chapter will now look more explicitly at these and other areas relating to pastoral care and worship. These suggestions are not meant to be a complete set or indeed 'the answer,' but they are offered as a way in. If the issue is raised, and reflection is made, whether or not one agrees with everything that has been written, then this booklet has served its purpose.

Shame is not purely an academic subject, and neither are people subjects or objects to be treated as such. We, the church, are a community of people who share the image of God. By having the courage to explore this issue further, we may grow in the knowledge of what that image means—who we are and who God is.

The Church

Teaching and Preaching on Shame
It is not often we hear and see studies or sermons on this issue. We often focus on sin as a personal issue, which induces guilt. How might shame be taught? How might an exploration into the subject that focuses on sin, identity, society expand the idea that we are all involved in this thing called 'shame'? One aspect can be that we examine the way we are all shaped as consumers—what does it mean to live a life that embraces another way of living? Will it mean that we are 'shamed'? How do we look at the issue of 'who we are' in society? What expectations do we impose upon ourselves and others? Are those expectations necessary?

Perhaps a focus on the biblical themes of reunion (Luke 15), citizenship (Eph 2.12–13), light (Col 1.15–20), wholeness (Gal 3.25–29), *shalom*, the kingdom of God, belonging—and many other types of metaphors and imagery—will bring a balance to a sin and guilt sermon series.

It also means that we get to grips with what type of God we are imaging in our preaching. Some classical icons of Christ can focus on the face and stress the connection with him through his eyes. This is not in order to feel condemned and shamed, but accepted and loved, understood and welcomed. Our preaching is a form of iconography. What image do we paint of God in our words and expressions? Do we encourage the listener to look at the eyes of Christ and feel welcomed or do we paint them in order to see them burning into our souls? Moreover what does the image of God we have tell us about ourselves, our weaknesses, or our views?

It is often in the preaching that we get an understanding of what the minister thinks—and not necessarily what the church thinks. But in the preaching we hear the 'shoulds' and the 'oughts.' We need to be very careful in expressing those 'shoulds' and 'oughts.' What other ways can be harnessed to encourage adoption of what we have taught? How aware are we of the demands we make upon our hearers every week?

Worship

Though many preachers would not like to admit it, much of the theology which people learn is not through the brilliant sermons, but through liturgy and most predominantly through the songs we sing. What are we saying when we sing? What theology or image of God is present in the hymns and songs we use every Sunday? Is it appropriate to think about other metaphors and images of God, if one is stressed above others? This may be a useful exercise in home groups and then ask each person what this image would imply.

Examples of songs and hymns that contain a movement from an abandoned, longing, fearful state to an accepted, loved and healed state are:

• *Father God I wonder*	• *When I survey*	• *God of grace*
• *My song is love unknown*	• *To be in your presence*	

Confession and Absolution

In what ways can a set or extempore confession be shaped that includes the vast mixture of feelings that we have when we come face to face with who we are? There is also a tendency to focus on sin and guilt, using biblical verses and liturgy to reinforce our need to confess. Shame then is simply an attachment to the feelings of guilt. Stephen Pattison writes that '[t]his prevents the fundamentally a-moral sense of shame from being recognized and addressed.'[18]

How can confession and absolution be a way of addressing our sinfulness yet at the same time stressing our goodness? We seem to be very good at emphasizing our badness yet ignoring that we were loved so much that God sent his only Son to give us life in abundance. The following confession from the Iona Community seeks to recognize the wounds that sin makes on ourselves and others—encompassing a wider understanding of our state. Priest and people repeat the prayer alternately:

> Before God, with the people of God,
> I confess to you my brokenness:
> to the ways I wound my life,
> the lives of others,
> and the life of the world.
> *May God forgive you, Christ renew you*
> *and the Spirit enable you to grow in love.*
> Amen.[19]

We could also try to stress the goodness of God's image within us, perhaps using language that signifies that image being marred. We could also stress that healing and wholeness are as much a part of Christ's work on the cross as forgiveness.

Atonement

Language of confession usually reflects a theology of the atonement. In lots of churches the main theory that is adopted and expressed as doctrine is 'penal substitution.' The continuation of this limits God and justice to a particular understanding of law and justice, thereby limiting God himself.[20]

All models of the atonement are partial and we must therefore be open to other insights, not to just one of them. In what ways can an exploration into the atonement recover a bigger picture of what God was doing? What images and language can help us to see shame as something that is addressed on the cross? We need to recover language that speaks of healing, reconciliation, liberation, transformation, restoration. In the midst of the shame that Jesus experienced in his suffering and the rejection of those around him we see Jesus embracing us in our own shame, in all the things we may have within us, that have been done to us. In the cross we see the possibility of humanity being transformed, the image of God being recovered and liberated so that we can be all who we are in Christ. On the cross Jesus embraces all of who we are—all our secrets, all our hiddenness, all our wounds, all our injustices, all our abuse of others and ourselves—and he brings wholeness.

The different theories of atonement do not negate the seriousness of sin, they seek to articulate all that sin is and does, all that shame is and does, all sins that we commit but also sins that are committed against us. On the cross Jesus was sinned against—yet he embraced that, so that there may be healing and forgiveness.

Breaking Down Boundaries

Jesus overturned the lawyer's understanding of 'neighbour' in Luke 10.25–37 when he showed that we ourselves define who is our neighbour. We are the ones that draw the boundaries between those we accept and those we do not. There are obvious groups within society that are excluded for various reasons—the poor, the refugee, the hounded. Such groups 'act as test cases for our hospitality.'[21] But there are also other forms of exclusion—which exemplify rejection and shame, a rejection of the person as not being needed or wanted. The person is not good enough or important enough. There are habits of exclusion that need to be tackled if the church is to reflect the glory of God. As Ireneaus once said, the glory of God is people fully alive, fully living.

Henri Nouwen writes:

> Much of our ministry is pervaded with judgments. Often quite unconsciously we classify people as very good, good, neutral, bad and very bad…Those whom we consider lazy, indifferent, hostile, or obnoxious, we treat as such, forcing them in this way to live up to our own views.[22]

So often we want people to 'behave' before they 'believe.' They have to be like us, they have to change what they are doing before they come to church. But the church is called to be a place where people are welcomed—where 'saints' and 'sinners' mingle. This means that we need to help people 'belong' before we ask them to 'believe,' and certainly before we ask them to behave! The church is called to be a community that is welcoming and accepting. That has an open door to all. We are called to accept people for who they are, not on the basis of what they have done or should do.

Mission
An understanding of shame may shape the way local churches do mission—the very act of welcoming and loving, the act of copying what God did in the Garden of Eden—going out to find, to look, to love, to heal. In what ways will it affect the message we take out? How can the language of shame—not just the language of guilt and forgiveness—be used to express the gospel? This is more so in overseas contexts where shame is a far more shaping factor of family and social living than here in the UK.[23]

Pastoral Support

Jean Vanier, founder of the L'Arche communities, wrote 'the health of a community can be measured by the quality of its welcome of the unexpected visitor.'[24] In many ways, pastoral support is connected to mission, as love is expressed to all who come in.

If anyone is in need of support, under the negative influence of shame, it is not just the minister who can help, but all can extend and, similarly, withdraw a welcome. There are some key areas to be thought about.

Identity
How people see themselves is crucial in the whole area of overcoming unhealthy shame. They need to move from the place of a negative self image to a healthy one; they need to see themselves as God sees them, through his eyes, and not through the eyes of the ones who have harmed them, abused, them, mistrusted them. Sebastian Moore writes:

> [r]eligion has done much more harm by endorsing people's wretched
> ideas of themselves, whereas it is precisely religion's job to cure people
> of this sin of self-negation.[25]

There are a number of ways this can be done, which all take time and a period of hard self-reflection. Done in companionship with a trusted person,
the shamed individual may come to a healthier image of who he or she is.
The questions below are a good place to begin but do not seek to be all that
is needed. In the cases of abuse and other more complex areas, professional
counselling must, of course, be offered as well.

Listen to the person and give real time and honour to him or her:
- What have been the chief voices or characters in the past?
- Can any negative incidents or moments be seen?
- Can any structures be seen that have caused shame?

Help the person see the difference between guilt and shame:
- Does sin need to be addressed?
- Has sin been committed against this person?
- Is there false guilt?

Help them see how God views them:
- What Bible passages can speak of God's view of us?
- How does God stress our essential goodness?

Our understanding of the 'new creation,' if used sensitively, can foster a hope
that within the person. The identity called into being by God, at conversion, is
able through the Spirit to live in the 'true identity' called for by being in Christ.
This should not promote a sense of guilt and shame, but of hope through
resting in God's grace. As we discover more about ourselves we learn that
the people we have always been trying to be may in fact have been people
created by others, not by God.

Love and Support
Our love needs to be expressed towards people as people, not as potential
pew fillers. Matthew 25.31–46 speaks of expressing love to the least—people
that have been excluded or forgotten. It reminds us that God calls us to love,
for God is love. It is in loving people as people that we discover Christ within
them. We do not love them as an altruistic way of loving God. In Matthew 25
Jesus speaks of two groups—those who did and those who did not love the
'least.' The difference is not that one saw Christ and the others did not; neither
saw Christ until the end. This knowledge of God and his incarnation in the
least did not initiate that love. It was love for the least—pure and simple. It
is in loving the least that we suddenly become aware and surprised of the

27

presence of Christ in them, not that we see Christ in them and then we can love them, for that is the mistake of the second group of people.

People with shame as a mantle covering them and extinguishing the light from them need to feel loved and accepted for who they are, not for who they can be or become. Our love for others begins with the now. The healing that can come from love will help them remove the mantle of shame, allowing them to be clothed in the white garments that God, who has been busy sewing them together, freely gives.

It is my prayer that this booklet will help all of us whose role it is to show life, in all its wounded experiences, to those whose lives are under shame; that by opening our eyes to what is around us, we will see through his eyes only, to be shaped by him only, so that all may have life and have it to the full; that God's glory will been seen in all its fullness.

Notes

1   All identities have been changed in this book.
2   Matthew Parris, *The Times* 4M, 19th July 2003, p 26.
3   Quoted in C D Schneider, 'Shame' in *Dictionary of Pastoral Care and Counselling* (Nashville: Abingdon Press, 1990) p 1162.
4   Thomas Scheff, *Microsociology: Discourse, Emotion and Social Structure* (Chicago and London: University of Chicago Press, 1990) p 169.
5   Jean-Paul Sartre, *Being and Nothingness* (London: Methuen, 1969).
6   M Lewis, *Shame: The Exposed Self* (New York: The Free Press, 1992) p 34.
7   Neil Pembroke, *The Art of Listening: Dialogue, Shame, and Pastoral Care* (Grand Rapids and Cambridge: Eerdmans, 2002) p 147.
8   Based on a diagram by Norman Krauss, *Jesus Christ Our Lord: Christology From a Disciples Perspective* (Scottdale, Penn: Herald, 1990) p 204.
9   David Ford, *The Shape of Living: Spiritual Directions for Everyday Life* (Grand Rapids: Baker Books, 2004) p 33.
10 *ibid* p 33
11 *ibid* p 44
12 E Erikson in 'Identity, Psychosocial' in David L Sills (ed), *International Encylopaedia of the Social Sciences* (1968) p 566.
13 Zygmunt Bauman, *Work, Consumerism and the New Poor* (Buckingham: Open University Press, 1998).
14 See Walter Brueggemann, *Genesis* (Interpretation; Atlanta: John Knox Press; 1982) pp 40–54.
15 Other include the healing of lepers and of blind Bartimeus.
16 Ched Myers, *Binding the Strong Man: A Political Reading of Mark's Story of Jesus* (New York: Orbis, 2000) p 202.
17 This is a phrase that I have developed to help illustrate what the healings signify — each has an additional element to its meaning other than simply a healing event.
18 Stephen Pattison, *Shame: Theory, Therapy, Theology* (Cambridge: Cambridge University Press 2000) p 248.
19 The Iona Community, *Iona Abbey Worship Book* (Glasgow: Wild Goose Publications, 2001) p 24.
20 A accessible study on the atonement can be found in Joel Green and Mark Baker, *Recovering the Scandal of the Cross: Atonement on New Testament and Contemporary Contexts* (Carlisle: Paternoster Press, 2003).
21 Ford 2004, p 42.
22 Henri Nouwen, *The Way of the Heart* (London: Darton, Longman & Todd, 1999) p 26.
23 See chapter 6 of Green and Baker, *Recovering the Scandal of the Cross*, for a good account of how the language of shame affects the message of the gospel in Japan.
24 Jean Vanier, *Community and Growth* (London: Darton, Longman & Todd, 2001) p 143.
25 Sebastian Moore, *The Fire and the Rose are One* (London: Darton, Longman & Todd, 1980) pp 68–69.